Matronymics

By the Same Author

Who by Water

Kate Ashton

Matronymics

Shearsman Books

First published in the United Kingdom in 2024 by
Shearsman Books Ltd
PO Box 4239
Swindon
SN3 9FN

Shearsman Books Ltd Registered Office
30–31 St. James Place, Mangotsfield, Bristol BS16 9JB
(this address not for correspondence)

www.shearsman.com

ISBN 978-1-84861-891-6

Copyright © Kate Ashton, 2024

The right of Kate Ashton to be identified as the author of this work
has been asserted by her in accordance with the
Copyrights, Designs and Patents Act of 1988.
All rights reserved.

Acknowledgements

Some poems in this collection have been previously published in print and online magazines, for which my thanks to the editor(s): 'for the boy who wept at Faure's Requiem', 'Rubens Red', 'missing' and 'A Minor Planet', in *Shearsman*; 'You lose a glove', 'Mother tongue' and 'the sound of music' in *Agenda*; 'face' and 'contraction' in *Causeway*; 'oracle' and 'Mary Does Laugh…' in *Fortnightly Review*; 'Father-horse' and 'Decalogue' in *Long Poem Magazine*; three sections of 'Matronymics' — 'genesis', 'words' and 'names' in *Molly Bloom*.

Tsjebbe Hettinga's 'Father-Horse' is from *It Faderpaard* (Bornmeer: 20 Leafdesdichten, 2014); Kate Ashton's translation appears here by kind permission the publisher, De Bezige Bij, Amsterdam.

My great thanks again to the poets Janet Sutherland and Lucy Hamilton, who read and provide all kinds of valuable input for my poems in progress.

I am lastingly indebted to Tony Frazer at Shearsman Books.

Contents

1. MATRONYMICS

the sound of music	9
Sprung	11
baklava	12
genesis	14
face	21
Laura	22
Ikon	24
You lose a glove	26
babushka's baby	28
Ewe	29
for the boy who wept at Fauré's Requiem	31
Mother tongue	33
Rubens Red	35
contraction	37
news	39
'Mary Does Laugh…'	43
missing	44

2. FATHER-HORSE

Father-horse	47

3. A MINOR PLANET

A Minor Planet	59
place	61
oracle	63
holy fool	66

travail in three stages	68
late late shows	70
The Convert	72
East Beach	73
Decalogue	76
Notes	85

part one

matronymics

the sound of music
for CR

and here she is as a giggling
girl long before she knew
who she would marry or
give birth to + and here she is

long afterwards laughing
because it was true and she
never knew all the things
that were wrong with her

sickness dire diagnosis all
those things the doctors
knew + she never knew dis-ease
so 'How are *you*?' she'd ask

before your worry could
get through before your
anxious daughter tone could
cross oceans by telephone

she never knew her sins
forgot small wanderings
until extreme unction
caught her confessionless

as ever bidding 'You go first'
and faced with such undying
faith the priest anointed her
with absolution in excess

of powers granted by his
vows + saw her put on immortal
when the trumpet blew
and heard at last what she

had loved to listen to + the
sound of music twice sung
in the flesh + once young
and once in aged blessedness

shared day by day without regard
for time or place or suffering
or pain or person near or far
or any worldly wrought dogma

Sprung

Yesterday the locksmith came for the front door, and while he was at it I asked him to break into your old mahogany chest, the one you kept in your bedroom where secret places were forbidden. Ivory-trimmed keyhole, little top left-hand drawer – one day after the carer left you locked it and threw away the key in case next time she stole the silver-backed hairbrush too, and grandma's comb and buttonhook embossed all down the handle

a single twist of spiral wire (where had he picked up such skills) and like a lepidopterist he loosed rare winged and sleep-lost things as never alit and pinned themselves at a hard breast; black bog-oak cocoon, carved consolation for a grief-clenched throat, a brooch of silver sixpences engraved 'AB'… C, D… whoever knew? amethysts for some slim wrist; truant enamel swallowtail red-eyed from fenland rains, silver rooster-mounted Cossack at the gallop from snow-wrapped Carpathia – carved combs, conch shells like old men's mouths strung toothless, spittle-flecked and wrung; arched back-scratcher, emery boards, file, scissor, chamois-shod buff; small opalescent pot of Mary Quant cuticle cream…

and pleated black a raven roost aloof from summer-skirted play, an unkindness of fans, sleek spines turned on female stuff… it was a boy he wanted all along, that husband of yours, an end to women, love, abandonment – and what good girls we were, each did his bidding, fled hearth and home, the one you'd made for us, blue plate and flowers on the table, went AWOL by boat or train or plane, or something slower

baklava

'know thyself' just
this sustenance

from humblest
most blessed and

ugliest of men
a simple truth

offered to all comers
on the square

each in their own
starved universe

as though hunger
for hope must

hunt from pole to
pole for so rare

a morsel short and
sweet sufficient

unto itself passed
to him *in uter*o

by midwife mother
from the wordless womb

a honeyed tongue
gift of the gods his

long denied
Dodekatheon

genesis

i
Who says the world awaits us warmly – to be
entered easily as a needle into yolk or single
butt of one smug sperm, the seedling's
stunned breakthrough, kippah awry
and gulping air? I
have languished long

in the shrieking cellar
and the silent room

where all forgetting is
accomplished.

Ask and it shall be given you – the pat
answer and the long stare. A-swoon
as beech that joyously breathes in
its bluebell antidote to spring
you shall beg for distraction
or respite before the search
for clues from sky-eyed
soothsayer patient
as the past

take today – I discovered my mother
just as though nothing had happened,
still inhabiting her unshared now
(how she lived among all those
chairs and crouching curs
I'll never know)

it was her way of erasing
pains and she had a great

many of them, all quite mad
and requiring medication:

give it another day the doctor
said then up the dosage send
her home to bake scones ah
how we loved her after-school
crumpets fork-toasted at the
hearth, hot buttered devoured
before they charred cratered
and spewing magma rancid as
the sisterhood –

we shall no longer tolerate
you men forever touching us
(me too) forever lapping up
the credit and the cash
we shall no longer
suffer it

or the aftermath

give us a big cut
along the belly
give us a cut

a little lower down   give us
a chance.

words
At twelve I came into the world
and I'll tell you what happened
when beauty beat its breast at

my door begging for entry
like a refugee head hung in
shame at its own suffering –

I admitted it – I could not help
thinking of wings, slight slender
darkness standing sentry on a
lane, prayer pulsing into flight,
furtive forgetful foraging
for home hung from
an attic beam –

while down below my mother
gave birth to words head-first
like doodlebugs... I'm still
defusing them as best I can
in this twilight, scrubbed,
gowned and gloved I
dissect away each stiff
unloved bruise-breasted
thing from nearby tissue –
winter lasts so long
up here almost
nothing survives it.

names
from the beginning we think
of names for things
how when why
we weigh them down with
whether

her womb is freighted
with will be her she
is ageless let her be
nameless and alone
in becoming

we make sure to take
what is ours to make into
tomorrow we say:
he is hours
she is hours

we may sacrifice
him to our god
pray

give us another one a
girl this time
to dress in spring
we shall call her
April

we will call her what
we will if it is all
the same to you

you are not family
you are not one
of us she shall
die young

legs akimbo a gushing
where the crown
should be

she shall not suffer much
it was normal back then
we gave them names
baptised them

gudesire gudewife
godspeed we wrote
them down
and now

we call her apoplexy
of the flesh poor unsexed
willing womb we
name her holy
Theotokos

ii
I did not love her half as much
as the mauve scabious for
example or bee orchid
or tremulous

anemone and later I
uprooted she who
wavered rootlessly
in her beauty
like lotus

adrift upon the world
volitionless as all places
of pilgrimage
and prayer

a pale altar I put her away
from me like sin I would
not succumb to flare
into fruit to

stare into that flawed fate you
could call it catastrophe
that would not be too
strong an image
ima

*mutter mama maman moeder
mem* memory she stoops
in the hall speaking
of dogs
and something
to eat

iii
you are still inconsolable
ravenous for a treat
neither hard nor soft
or warm nor quite
so cold

let go she holds me
close like unasked
relinquishment
dire patterned
on the past

I call her sky-lynched
apocalypse of the mind
lost couch high

dereliction I
always
did my best

for you madman he cries
out cloud-clad cataclysm
mesmerised madonna
arboured among
monks

purged of impurity by
some sin-seared priest
sculptress of air
she reeks

of frankincense and
her toes are bare
they touch her
everywhere

sometimes she is sold
I knew her by her old
name: *untold*

veiled in obsidian purdah
hidden as her hair pinned
up between dark galaxies

hear our entreaties you
can hardly reach us now
you see we've roamed
so far from home

face
for Jo

Repulse Bay, hot March Sunday afternoon,
stilled dragon drowse above the holed
dream view of laden leaden sea, sun-
sodden crowds, she calls a taxi.

Young gwailou pair semiclothed bold
holding hands, keen to get back to city
bed soonest and no kidding
jump the queue, jump in,

my baby-bellied daughter-in-law
sprints, apprehends the car, hauls
open a door and now she's
so far away I can't hear

what it is she yells, fierce flare red
outrage on the air, six months
gone, small hotfoot son
left staring on the pavement –

feng shui master say: *no building there,
high peak his home, he must come and go* –

a dragon gate, an architrave, space
through which respect may flow
to placate destiny, save face,
honour wind-water harmony.

Laura

SILICA
The mental state is peculiar. The patient lacks stamina. What Silica is to the stalk of grain in the field, it is to the human mind. Take the glossy, stiff, outer covering of a stalk of grain and examine it, and you will realise with what firmness it supports the head of grain until it ripens; there is a gradual deposit of Silica in it to give it stamina. So it is with the mind; when the mind needs Silica it is in a state of weakness, embarrassment, dread, a state of yielding.
            Lectures on Homeopathic Materia Medica, James Tyler Kent, 1905

symptoms and sensations

singing	as of stroked glass rim
ringing	as of same lightly tapped
weeping	as of rain on skylight
shattering	as in shivery disorder
withdrawal	as in mute refusal
compliance	as in meek assent
lambent heat	as in flushing of the skin
clairvoyance	as in seeing

through
transparency
inner tensile strength
outer fragility

mental
love of clarity   preference for the   clear
company of creatures breath-blown a-graze
in crystal field and glade spindle-limbed
and lost from kin

need to groom
unbroken colt   handle
with care
the molten memory
that bolts the soul   replace

on the shelf
each brittle solitude

generalities
enervation after exertion

peculiar
feels she is the only one
who hears
the moonstruck cry
of light
on quartz

that finds the inner flaw –
like Mother's plea
for her to greet
gentleman caller
at the door

Ikon

Sometimes I dwell on first principles,
the solemnity of yes, its gravitas, or the
day that brings in the month of May,
how it hovers between now and then
keen to seduce the clenched calyx despite
foreknowledge of night snow, slow white
on grey, how it lays down betrayal

not anyone knows which way to turn but
seeks direction by despair, coercion, *fait
d'accompli*, chance signpost by the path –
most tampered with – how assiduous
the trace of fortune in the palm, collation
of exactitudes to graze, to perjure
fate, they are a hapless race –

who was present at the birth of blue, I
ask? who lit love of parabola on starling
wing? they cannot listen for loneliness, they
cannot see for surfeit, it is the saddest thing –
I put myself beneath them, I do not need
their prayers, their obeisance appals me –
all my desire is loss of levity

weight at the waist, fullness where they
play at the breast, no more assay but in its place
collected wit, unwritten liturgy, bowed heads
and unhurt hearts – uncounted they who wet
my hem with tears before the earth began
to lose itself beneath their tread for
heaviness, for sorrow –

I have wrung out my woad into the sea,
annulled their lamentations, their plaints
repel me – give me instead dusk's gilded flit
of pipistrelle, a thrill of cherubim, careless
crescendo of flung flow – do not dare depose
me from my throne of flesh, this earthy seat
the bower of my worldliness –

what are your fears to me? a shudder
where your faith should be, unuttered
tongueless terror of tomorrow, do you know
you have it in you to let go? and fathomless
this fall, to tend the brow bruised by a thousand
kisses that foreshadow yours, sored by
petitions still to come – how all endless

You lose a glove

You lose a glove you think
I truly lost it way back
then you say

something fell you
say how your fingers
lay crouched against

the crimson darkness upside
down and knitted like
fontanelle you think

nobody said it would be
like this so excruciating
stitch upon stitch you

think how a mitten paws
the path and gasps and sucks
at puddles unsure

alone and indolent
ungrown stillborn no
longer warm

you search the wheaten
dunes for you
and all along

the snowdropped edge
of spring where soon
the burrowed

sandpiper will soothe
to sleep her sky-shy
fledging and find

beneath each folded
wing the memory
of suffering

the way you lost
a sister on a walk or
while you sat to read a book

as though time took
back what it most missed
without good reason

or regret as though to
show the ease of it the
nostrum for forgetfulness

babushka's baby

she took her belly to the gynaecologist told him to save the child while speechless medics scraped out Ukrainian wombs and the authorities stayed mum for six whole days

tap water ran radioactive cow's milk too Strontium-ninety in the grass half-life of nearly three decades – all better now (for all we know) Easter thirty years on grandmothers picnic

beside the spating River Ness she tells of weeks flat on her back to keep her son inside… no outdoor play for mine either all through his spring holiday two thousand miles away

north-west of Kiev you couldn't eat the chanterelle or spinach from the market… and her Ilyin born pelted in black hair took years to learn to talk and her home town still hushed by

blood infanticide and both our boys fathers now we live on in the air that does not know decay but bathes water-borne spore revivifies the yolky gill and sleeps between the folds

of each half-born and foraged thing

Ewe
i.m. Gerrit Offringa (1943–2019)

He climbs the steep dyke steps, a
farmer's son, rolls and lights a cigarette,
on either side spring grassed misty
slope scented sheep-dug clod

seeded with dung still now as then
when he fled home for fields of shallow sea,
searched long low shore for mother-
of-pearl in shell-wept lagoon locked

tight between mudflats awaiting inundation
soon by flow the way all things must go,
height to meek mud, erasure then rebirth
by beak, breast, wind, wing, sky-flung

epiphany. He breaches the rise, first
glimpse of far slipstream between
sandbank and monk-made isle – the ewe
stands humped and huge

and truculent and bars his path, gaze divided
horizontally between derision and despair –
nonplussed he stares at such intent, fearless,
immovable, ram-like or like a man

she nudges hard, blunt-browed and will
not budge until he lets her lead him back
down where in the lee a brackish pool
lies deep and brown and drowning

at its reedy edge her rush-kneed stumbled
truant lamb surprised by the faint swell,
drench flanked, slow rowing hooves
and tongue-tied as a scolded son.

for the boy who wept at Fauré's Requiem

i
borage blue sky unclouded as cobalt
eye old stone fenestrate place
star

smitten upturned face glazed gold azure
dazed cherubim swum troubled
jade

of inturned sea caught piteously pray
for me a little birth a lamb low
born

ii
in blood and snow opal apostle
fist of flame names Jack James
Stephen

Latin carved in old black oak aback
white lace framed face
sinless

iii
as love's plainsong a prayer
flown apse altarless bare
as ages stripped

iv
of singing stone echoing holy
Mary muse a requiem
for them a

men again a Kyrie eleison a son
a mother seated in the choir
calm beauty

v
beneath reaching roof
of upturned ark steep
stern drop

dream deep drown the boy
is lost at sea head bowed
suddenly she

sees he is weeping averts her gaze
preserves his dignity he
rubs his eyes ten

vi
years eleven maybe I see
he gives me glass he
gives me sliding

river flow sepia light above
shy upturned glaze of stone
and dispensation

at last he gives me grace to melt
like glass-eyed sky or sealed
sepulchre of salt

vii
become rainbow sprung cell
sung open as the Book
of Life itself

Mother tongue

It's not that the gate was left open
but what has passed through –
tides of lapis lazuli
jade sways of sea
and spring after spring the doe that bows
beneath lichened ash bough the colour
of her hide

we always knew new life would come
of it until last year's
full flower moon
hung luscious as
ripe apricot a blush that shrank from touch
filled mouths with Tantalean watering
and outright shame

at first they came with babes in arms
sweet suckling sons and
daughters drenched in
desert dust and
oud and shimmering they came eyes kohled
and turned aside from our crude insolence
and flagrant lies

what overcame us then was ancient:
they crept ashore bowed low
before us on
bare knees like old
wisdom open at the page we'd closed
the day we lost our sight of things to come
as was foretold

some said it was nothing but old news
no truth but rumour
feeling its way
like fate or some
lost traveller apostate mired in myth
apocrypha afloat on unclean air
like vagrant motes

we felt the darkling spin of space move in
to steal our breath away
lostness beyond
hope like letting
go of some safe hold on worlds beyond
ravenous reach of entropy and grief
some certain home

they spoke old tongues we did not know
held fast to their beliefs
knelt to the stone
that holy place
with hands open in prayer the way
they read the Book of Truth
of everywhere

we looked into their eyes to find ourselves
unclothed as dethroned deities
aloof itinerants
who faced iconoclasm
at the gate because we'd lost
the words for womb for welcome
and good faith

Rubens Red

Something Flemish maybe, weight,
ornate gilt-listed looking-glass, high
ceiling cornice swagged and bare
pale cluster at the rose

or was it the Grassmarket's open
throat, a-glitter gasp of last repose,
a scintillating perfumed pulse
echo of emptied artery,

no urgency, no force, Grande Place
forgetful of its double tongue,
true iteration of the wooded
edge where once the doe

indelibly described her arc
and night transcribed it into
trembled time as slow
processions of leapt dark –

or perhaps felled stand of onyx
flesh, architrave crowned with
outraged frown, small footfall
in mid-air, clawed cheek,

lost clutch, hot bloodless breast
that mourns itself to stony
death, long loosed locks become
shriek-shroud for bluing son,

too much milky measure hurled
headlong into silken lap where
no cry holds, a stifled slide through
carmine pleat and fold –

and then Kaddish between the thighs,
soft intimation of desire, blank
affirmation mirrored in the hall,
slow dawning crimson climb

as step by step in its own time
bright spill made spate sure as all
destiny, something fulfilled,
another fate than mine.

contraction

we're on the stairs now and all the hours
piled up behind us she says no
no more she says

no

more

and down the outside stairs we go
one tread at a time and between them the long   no
and her face facing down into the next
hand flat on hard beneath
hard breasts her pressing hand

the pressing face the face pressed
flat against traced place that she can't see   a little rose
a Catherine window tightly mullioned
where no light shows
and no

to breathing no to go   and no   to
whatever is to come and no
to whatever is gone   time
punched out like paper holes
raw-edged white and

incandescent somehow

don't talk to me no
it is not fine it is no

you bastards fuck your it's
okay and you are doing
fine fuck you too   little
too big   too late   too slow   too long   too

nothing

happening

big strong heavy thing   get it out
no you
do it

it'll all be over soon sit
in the front no you sit there here hold
my hand tight a no all running everywhere
inside a huge and
nothing in it

soon be over soon
very soon now
breathe count   one   two
doing fine down
there all gone

no

more no

so

white

do you want to see your beautiful

no

news

sunset
where is her god – this
ruined goldilocks in lemon

yellow stilettos? black
cat-suit of the tv news a

camera pans down long crossed
legs – i watch a small grey

mewling leap from bling
bloused breast into another

mother's arms swim the plaited
confluence of pain that streams

between us – lady do not adjust
your seamless privilege or tweak

common complicity this more
than naked barbarity why do i

buddha here consuming
you as tranquil evening falls

why vicariously feast on
death-strewn foreign

afterlife from a safe distance –
in truth i like my dead

hygienically embalmed a good
few litres of formaldehyde a

touch of panstick to the cheek
to expunge recent history (may

god forgive our pacifist
scruples) young Magdalene

struts the rubbled streets
beauty routine intact

especially in times like these
it makes her feel much better

pink fake Versace bag and
matching anorak

*you may find some images in our
report distressing* – pour me another

mother of the silver scream i
love your outfit and your lip

wish us goodnight it's not too late get
home and kiss your little one sleep tight

nocturne
i bet your house has working
walls and doors and windows

about that
cat though

i have news for you it
knows on which side its saucer sits

does not care for cameras
at the final checkpoint –

child drained of all but dream
small home drawn on backseat

screen warm cat in commaed nap
prayer scrawled on mummy's

map *where does
this road end*

go on ask her how she feels
i need more grief

fresh wept to rinse away
this nameless shame a

ten-year-old seeks water
on recaptured street

my heart is more at peace
his mother clasps his hand

remarks with a wry smile *so
much fear* she stoops

lies off the scale!
scoops up a wide-eyed

guileless sixth or seventh life
(*may it be blessed my Lord*)

she will convey it from the long
unlove where men scavenge

for sons in pinewood
dell where forages

the faceless omnivore
for more night-ripe

at forest edge and gran digs
in her heels hides loss

behind grime-nailed iconostas
and lights incense to

lay to rest late season's
venal stench – so who's

to blame this time if I may ask
a fellow felon dressed

to kill – whose fault the guys
make war while

we make more babies – well
to be fair we job share

unbelievable the
cost of childcare

'Mary Does Laugh...'
i.m. Sister Corita Kent (1918–1986)

...goes to Tesco for tinned soup,
shops savvy – Campbell's
three-for-one (father, son, and so on),
damns the ready-meals to hell,

gets mad, stays off message ever
since the feral one-off incident
presaged by that weirdo with wings
landed her in the ordure

goes on all the demos, ducks the
iPhone selfies and a fallen angel
or two: '*buy more, make more war,
fuck up the world for good and all...*'

the sons of men they come and go,
Mother Mary is the juiciest tomato.

missing

here is white   feel
how unequivocal   how
the land bequeaths its own
reply   asks nothing   how
hungrily it   cleaves
where time forgets itself
in some sort of

bliss here on the hard
earth   which recalls
no insult   come in
do not ask why

do not say   I do
not understand   these words
what do they mean?
they mean to

obliterate you   soon
at Imbolc   beneath a
bright storm-moon
on lambing snow

spring
where Bridget's green
rush crosses grow   overwept
with white   and aconite's
gold coronet

foretells sudden   demise
undreamt of yet   how good to
rest   welcome

none will affright you   we
are close as kin   to tender
night   its thin embrace
frontierless

there is no cure   but   solace
for the   fall   forget
yourself   deep grief
is kind for all

recall
it has mislaid   its memory
of taste   soft skin   like
you   seeks south   asks
which way for

touch of him   relief at
unuanced   mouth   lips
unversed in   artifice
or guile

longs for   nothing   more
nor less than lost
truth   light shawl
cats-paw

warm   slid   over claw
to hold off   hostilities
uncalled for
catastrophe

loss
arrived on tiptoe   sent
ahead   awaited like
like some wingless
messenger   do

not look for signs   sad
necromancer   follow your
god   or the blind angle
of the sun

no one need know   where
you come from   are
bound   or whether
white awaits you

patiently   at some long
hour in the flat   hinterland   this
loss of things like winter
it is home

Part two

Father-horse

by

Tsjebbe Hettinga

Translated by Kate Ashton,
finalised with Gerrit Offringa, 2016–2017

from *It Faderpaard*,
by Tsjebbe Hettinga
(Bornmeer, 2014)

The poet and musician Tsjebbe Hettinga was born in 1949 into a large family, on a farm just outside the village of Bolswert in the southwest of the Dutch Province of Friesland. His father bred cattle and Frisian horses. By his late teens an hereditary condition had begun to rob Tsjebbe of his eyesight, and in adulthood he was completely blind, writing by dictation and sing-speaking his poems from memory at readings. I first encountered this poet's richly ornamented, profoundly emotional poems while living in Friesland, where he is greatly revered. He was virtually unknown beyond his homeland until the 1993 Frankfurt Book Fair focused on Dutch literature and Hettinga took the stage for the first time before an international audience; his 'reading' caused a sensation.

In Friesland I was enthralled by stories of him related by mutual friends and acquaintances, and by recordings of his voice and saxophone playing – but never met him myself. Then in 2013, ten years after moving home to Scotland, I learnt online of his death and was shocked at the loss of that voice to the world. I began translating the epic sequence *It Faderpaard* more to console myself than with any thought of publication. The poem, dedicated to the poet's father, is a eulogy for a real colt who grew into a stallion so majestic, intelligent, loyal and loving that he stole his breeder's heart – the farmer fought his passion, selling the beautiful creature again and again and each time buying him back for more money. Such a lapse in business ethos is entirely foreign to the famously pragmatic Frisians. But finally the stallion was bought home for good by the farmer's son and heir, to draw his father's funeral coach.

In Hettinga's glorious free interweaving of time, myth, locality and legend I recognised his love for Dylan Thomas (he translated *Fern Hill* into Frisian). I wanted to stay close to the form and structure Tsjebbe had chosen for his sequence, its rich alliteration and other-worldly imagery; and to emphasise and play on the linguistic kinship between the Frisian and English languages. I was not (capable of or) aiming for an academically approved translation, but for a faithful rendition of the extraordinary depth, emotional power and cinematic scope of this sightless poet's inner world.

*Frisian stallion; photo copyright © Carmelka, 2014.
Via iStockphoto.com*

Father-horse
for Piter Mebius Hettinga (1916–1993)

I
Tomorrow it will be eternal spring, but now it is night.
The moon – the soul of one who dies in the dark –
Is full, and drunken as the paths between villages, above
Black pyramids of farms, the pitch-black pointing fingers
Of God's houses, and a purple car bonnet
Hurled towards the father horse in his blinkered
Stallion stall, in a last breath of wind, beneath the stars.
Across the field of birth, ripening may be heard, and
Above the bent-backed coach house with a black-lacquered
Tilbury stands Venus waiting for her night-black stud
Soon to arise from sea-salt byre as in a dream, flooded in light.

Listen. Blinded by the flare, a seventy-year-old dog goes mad,
Breaks loose from his blue chain that's consumed in silver
Flames and snap-snatches at high-held fetlocks that
Heavy in black hair dance free of the green paddock.
The crack of a whip – it's forefather, father – rings
In the pricked ears of a wind-still farm, in the seven
Twin shells that belong to a child a-gasp for clouds.
And a roar, ur-beast deep, coupled at once with
The glad pleading of voluptuous mares, court-keen
In spring's resounding stable, leaps fences
Into the dew-wet field that brims with unsolved secrets,

Until within the devout toll-holes of far submissive
Temples and the stone lion of the southwest where
The stubborn bells of the world are stilled by it,
And silenced. Time a horse, and wooden clogs, blush
Red, whipped up into a frenzy like wind-painted elms
Surrounding a flushed apple-hoard, take new grass
Galloping home, harness horses foaming, sweat-silvered

And pulling at the traces; cartloads of love's faith in the flesh.
And again, a deep clarion call; impossible to hold,
It flies out by night along the street to the prancing
Dance of villages demanding the earth of an angel, and

See, lily-light the face, grey-green the eyes, huge and
Black as night's high stabling the tidal swell of hair;
Clog slippers glimmering jet as boot-blacked hooves
On high-flying horse-show days carry cattish
Class that flirts and flounces in twirling Charleston;
And over a love-misted macadam road beneath
The whirling wheel of moon there frisks a grass-green
Hungry pair (through whiff of horse or cow across
Their path) towards an apple orchard under falling stars.
And a first 'Oh' from so nearby breaks open a sky –
Is that echo a Harley? – and riding over hot clouds, horse.

From marshy mud shallow the stallion shoots into sight,
As though carved from sea clay by dawn's misty
Maids, he stands there: wade withers, thighs higher
Than the breasts of dunes, flanks, muscles, tighter than
The blue line of northern horizon, the wild plain
Of his back, saga of the soothing neck that in the myth
Of his black mistral vanishes, and the lusts
Of a tail proud planted treelike in the flesh;
And fine head in the clouds, gaze run aground
In a mare's eyes, he flees the flight of dancing hair,
Hunts her half down to death and leaps, flooding into her tide.

And snuffing the salt of a stall, he struts, strides dapper
Down the wide hay-tinted shore, past sucking
Salt marsh in grass-green glory of growing.
Held and haltered to the waxing moon, a moon
Full of prayers and rocking on the swell,
Spring forth blue foals like flying fish that cabriole

From oceans. A black mare snickers lip trilling beneath
Harvest's laundered cumuli, and runs through
Ring-tilting seaside villages with a black lacquered
Tilbury that sets the evening glittering in scents
Of leather, carbide, gin, and unbridled stallion.

That steed who strikes macadam from the streets, sways
Blinkered hamlets in a dream of heaven-sail towards
The vast balloon of a moon that glides across
The sea, voyages on in love along a lane that leads
To a sea-salt stall with gilded yellow sea-straw bed and
The sea that shines on and on, plunging on its way. Away.
And the spokes in the wheel of foal-full black lacquered
Summer night turn in their round-rush slowly
Back in the light of time-splintering stars. And stallion
And Venus ride, ride through the night of now, because
Forever and ever it has been eternal spring, forever, ever.

II
Tonight it will be eternal night, now that in the fragile
Mirrors of memory spring escapes the light
And eyes cloud in the head, in becalmed
Farmstead where like a blind planet a soul circles
That finds the doors slammed shut, windows blinded
With horse hide; bony fingers that reach for field full
Of blood-red sorrel, feel the dark dust of worm-
Riddled collar-beam in the last grains of gravelly light;
And beneath roof tiles with the dead birds, creaks
More softly than the spiders in their inky webs
A tracery of timber grounded in the sea-salt earth.

And above the glazed hayloft where memories are
Dumped, there flutters through a barn afloat on dust
The dazed bat of despair; hidden in tongues of flame

Lamenting lips drop through the trapdoors
Of a high silage-store where long black locks lie twined,
Faded lilies and a child's toy with soot-stained window
Panes; and carried on the wings of fate, a stuffed crow
Bearing in its dusty beak a peacock plume bouquet
Forewings it through the grotto of the little byre
Towards a pitch-black Harley, and a leather-clad lad,
Cylinder-head, fumbles for a farm lass, a helmet

That hangs dust-filled in the hayloft of the big
Barn on the eye of a beam that speaks proverbs:
'No greater grief than to recall joy in a time
Of sorrow'. And the soul wanders on like the sheen
Of a dark moon into the derelict homestead.
On trembling daub walls hang workhorses, done in,
Done for; and a circus pony in its hellish piste
Agape at the breath of trapeze artiste, falling,
Turning top to toe into a black felt cocoon; and
Fingers reach for rings to clasp the wrists during
The dance of death, for necks, for bony skeleton

To soothe beneath hot breath on earth, on grass, in air, and
An all-devouring fire sparks, flares from the ashy
Loins of an old love, an inferno that with a final 'Oh'
Razes the farmstead to the ground; and speech-drowned
In his sea-bound stall the stallion breaks loose, crazed
By the fury of the flames, kicks pitch-pine from partition,
From wind-side door, and from his tarry crèche
Flees with neck collared as though iron-shoe shod,
Black feathered hooves that scud salt sea clod
From dead furrow, tears of earth that fall to earth
Slant through the hard-stretched souls of the sea back

To the sea. Night a horse, and the long black manes
On his blinkered flight past the stricken belfries

Of an earth-dark age, losing the kingly barrows
Of a once dug place, he appears suddenly on
On an ashen shore, and on and on to where
The swamps of aeons suck and draw. And
Deeper and deeper he sinks slowly in salt silt
And clay back past his mythic thicket of whiskers, his
Soft beloved muzzle, praying lips: *and it shall be dark,*
Until out from the cobwebbed coach house of a dream
A black-lacquered tilbury clatters blind-eyed for the road

In leaps and bounds: the wheel of the moon shall creak and
At the crowing light the dog go barking mad; the farm
Shall whinny, enthralled at the twinkling of the dew
And the doors swing open for the swallows
And the swaying horses; now let the sun swagger through
The fields, and grass in rapture recall youth's innocence;
Let the south wind spread the far tower's early hour
Across the timeless pastures, and let pleasure arrive
Like a distant friend, robed in tales of elegance and woe;
Let the unfettered horses gambol then, and roll
In sunlight's rising warmth, let the colts leap and

Startle, flee and halt to drink at milky clouds,
Let the children burst free from the green village
To chase hares and an ever-blue breeze
In the grassy perfume of free afternoon, and let
The sun that sails from sea to shore sink calmly
Into sorry-saying's sprung stable; let the day
Thus run its course and evening come on russet wings;
Let the spirit not be weighed down with cups of vanity,
Let laughter belong not solely to the other, or grief
Either; let come the silence, the night, the dream, and
Let in the seekers, those who have sought, for the light.

part three

a minor planet

A Minor Planet

Next time I will be born not on a planet, but on a comet!
　　—Marina Tsvetaeva (1892–1941)

Too much – too-muchness – that's
what sent you running, my
hunger for truant Jewish
fathomlessness –

words – sprung from your lips
like irreducible first truth,
old tender writ fit to
annihilate the world –

it was you stupefied my past –
first loss that chars to ash first
love, you who knew what lay ahead,
life's homelessness –

such peerless nights! pale brow
like moonstruck snow and on
your face all earth's repose –
already you were far

from me – I should have seen
the augury – dead daughter, famine,
din – war's feckless common tongue,
cacophonous, obscene –

too much!

always the same over-exuberance
of love or hate doled out some
reckless where or way – soul
over-shown – the shame!

then trains, treeless tundra
chill, day after day we froze –

he was still only a boy but so
tall, so brazen, and what sort

of mother was I anyway
for such a son?

place

razed village, ravage, she flees,
stumbles unrobed undone, on
her retina a scarred negative
of those too old to run

arrives in some far place where
the stranger takes her in, he
who fled south for a better life,
she a girl to wash to bed as wife,

hair charred silk upon his skin,
eyes fire-flecked tiger-stone, breath
sweet as lychee on his tongue,
young womb to welcome

sons and daughters born
auspiciously with a new moon
for beauty *jyutping*, good fortune –
soon the new young widow

leaves his house, walks north
through borderlands to bow
to the first wife, show face
accept the guest water

and rice – here is the home
of crimson *cheongsam*, dragon
fruit flaring at the shrine like
sweet shriven lunar fate

fallen to earth where red wife
plants feet wide, awaits her due,
pink wife stoops low with
downcast eyes, crawls through

oracle

i
they did not choose beauty
knew that soon kouros
would shake off melancholy

stance awake foot forward
ravishing and tender-toed a
sweet-kneed sprinter made

to outrun time – they saw to
one another's needs – love
plunged across the isthmus

ii
(these were the days of awe
we fasted on the pinewood
path fought our new wars
forgiveness far behind us)

iii
they did not choose youth
for yearlessness is fey – rather
a plain matron farsighted

as fecundity and grey –
how I wept to see young
priestesses like cyclamen

flee sanctuary and shrine
flush-cheeked trailing the veil
in terror of today –

for I do not deal in plain
speech – why should I
given an age of plethora?

so many words for stone
yet voiceless primeval mute
architect of peak and slope

it haunts the air refusing
to be spoken – only dare
walk where in an instant

it is not where ancient chelonian
plays rock beside the rift
quilted in quiet centuries

dwell on long absence from
this hill how haste delayed
ascent drift hid the cleft

and ravenous crevasse – you
know all is not as it seems
slow exodus decks the ravine

iv
they did not choose virginity
once understood the hunger
for despoilment they knew

a seasoned womb transmits
unabashed raw wisdom
of the marriage bed they

did not disdain the sway
of bay upon the intellect
displacement of the thirst

to know for feral trance
unsullied interlude of grace –
only approach this place

stilled abyss at the centre
of the world where hums
and shakes inchoate word –

v
one day they embraced shame
mistaking god for son – swore
to cut out my red drenched

tongue I spoke openly then of
raped adyton quenched spring
woe on a warring world of men

holy fool

because she erred i clung to signs of mute angel and metaphor. seems
she did not know what she did or so they tell me she didn't mean it

i tend to know what i did but there you go – everyone's different. i do
this and i do that and mostly bad. and mostly i mean it. still

so cruel – those silk-slippered defections
i saw where the oar left its spoor in fast

flow how wide water portrayed perilous hope lay open to soft azure
rape. she always stole from me mostly bits of soul made them her own
and retold me

anyway what does it matter what she knew? she flew too close to the
polar opposite of love maybe due to lost meridian misread ingress – or
else she

lived in ignorance of her own strength
or else knew far too much of it – fact is

that in the tremor of a quill she taught me very littleness. as for
unknowing – like a doubly discovered lie i like it very much. it quite
suffices

like *sans*
like *in extremis*

try to shamble as I do – just try it you won't be able to. you're too cool.
hey look out for brilliance! for instance bamboo snake. stop keep still
– watch glory cross your

path. far too easy to die of sullied circumstance – multitudes have and
that's the horror of it. they do not see my lovely seraphim

but go about and make
a great success of things

o blue soaked world stroked silk bark bleach of silver birch thin purity
of agonisingly peeled skin how breezily they sing and douse themselves
in gilt

as lifelong twins yet
all seem in cahoots

or more or less seem to think they are. strange surety. not anywhere i
tread is certainly intact. not any floor or surface. well some things have
to change

look at my feet – nice felt mules
eh? a long time since she left

for peekaboo oblivion. some sunsets i espy her in my bird-brained space
and then i take flight again wahoo in why-winged murmuration

travail in three stages

first
like a visor before the face they wore
sentiment to hide their scars – somewhere
they had planted things in an unremembered
how or when, the firstborn of their sorrows.
I kept on meeting them –

snow lay in the dunes where fireweed lit
the winter memory with javelins of magenta
light – each upright stalk was now adorned with curls
frigid as shriven words mouthed by the widower
bearded sparse and grey

but I could not forget cerise, tall crowds that thronged
the mound where the mad poetess was run to ground –
milk left upon the table – I knew tomorrow would
bring more of them, some I recognised,
I saw to flee was futile

second
a little into thaw I scraped the plot the way they clean
an endometrium of commaed spot – it was consensual

but cruel, the light it shed on nakedness and truth – a place
that does not know itself but innocently waits and cedes
itself in purge of grief at unpaid debt, the pricelessness

of what is let and wasted purpose – such insight was new to me
and was not welcome – the others saw my state, their spit was soon

upon my face, they viewed my vacant belly with contempt – disgraced
I scanned the the hollow where pink fire had flared
but all was bled – I could not find myself in this

unshared history passed womb to womb like some strange
malady too bestial or beauteous to be told – what kind of past

resists relay or insistent escape? the men who came upon
me then marked rare absence of self-regard, took
what was left and cast the carcass by the path

third
At last I tried to set a seed but out of common season – inclemency
and anguish grew and all my kin were gone ahead leaving no word –
I felt the soundless surge – smelt milky breath – stepped down into
extremity where life and death share same sained hearth – until the
bloodstained cinder bed unfurled a still small rebirth of the world

late late shows
for Martha Argerich, pianist, 1940–

a hotel breakfast plate late fruits vibrate nasturtium   my mother's ageing sightless face   as imperturbable as death   that child who slaved at the piano   how I longed to be a doctor   the trouble is I work too much   travel too much have no one for whom I   am   important   a man?   yes   love that's unattainable   Chopin   the soul that's difficult to touch   I loved your father in a very interior way not very lyrical he says   too passionate   not light enough   too

serious   he loves beautiful women   the ones who float on air   and I don't laugh enough because everything is blah blah, blah   but sit in the grass while his daughter paints my big toenail blue   she has loved my feet since long ago   she crept between the pedals while I played   I don't want them all done in the same shade   my desire has always been to create confusion   how do I feel about this   becoming seventy?   maybe I'll be a little bit scared

where shall I want to live? toes so homeless they know the priestless liturgy   the limbless minim   lovely mistress of kenosis   repetition fugue   crescendo   no use to speak of notes   explain what you feel   each movement of the soul   but continue discovering work   listen   it's difficult   ennui does not exist for me   the thing is not to imitate oneself not get worse   less fresh   I

wanted to be alone   for two years I did nothing drank beer travelled watched late late shows the baby did not seem to belong to me   I felt more like a big sister you know   bizarre   I was overwhelmed I had her against the odds   I've no idea why   I   refused to visit her   or that mother maladroit of mine   she also smoked most strange   she held the cigarette so huge hands   she'd always wished they held healing power less mother more a   sort of

friend exotic confidant Madame Chiang Kai-shek in shades   ashamed of so lawless a daughter   her mother not the kind of grandma who made jam   more the sort who caused storms   where to live?   not anywhere   a worry to me now   the wordless worldless domicile   utmost exile where I cling by my fingertips   and worse my counterfeit performance other-where   what can I say daughter pianissimo   I

love being near   you
bizarre   this   frenzied
passion for escape   rehearsal
of lost things   sentinelle
perdue   ashen in the wings

The Convert
Eric Gill, wood engraving, 1925

how light he leans
into the torrent of her dress
toe-trips fast
flowing folds notes
high unhidden breast

waltz-holds her waist
unripe moonrise between
his thighs draws
down the swell
beneath his touch

to wolf one flooded
sun eyes wide upon
her upturned face

trim to the gunwales wades
the night crazed waters
of her praise

East Beach
for Catherine

salt fretted touch on us
fretful untamed
and we each recoil
recall slow
sway

how we went woman's unsung way of war
of unconditional surrender and all

for hard winnings as they always are
quick or moribund hours for the keeping

sometimes a souvenir
of anguished brevity
or cruel
reversal of
first law

(how infinitely small how weighty those must be
oh how much lighter than a scattering of light)

loss like an unchosen
never was
or frost blight on
first rose

and what of we who force
the lock on memory
by dint of unearned
grace of grievous
innocence

fate
as futureless
and stripped of rank
or name we
march

on our way to new
nomenclature in
fearsome grip
of dark (*all right down there?*)
that slips

genes onto macramé
thread until
like grandmama
we darn
the past

and small wonder what with the visiting of sins
upon the sons – it's more than anyone can bear

salt
being the primal taste of child upon the tongue
the way they know what's to be done their

impossible insouciance
their *now!*
and how we
come
into being on

the back of him while he lies on the racked slack belly
laying down the law – all mouth and moral scruples

okay! keep your hair on
I'm on my way
fanned foam outrun
where brine
comes in

like milk where we must again become some common heroine
bathed in beginnings – bare-toe the sharp-strewn memory

the chill retreat and clutch
and glory
of it all

then doesn't she
just stop stock-still
and get the tide

to recite *The Lord's Prayer*
in the Irish
and even a *Hail Mary*

Decalogue
after Krzysztof Kieślowski

i

All that breaks the matrix –
without lineage or temple
bell save for spring pine's
sweet censer swing where
bees beg pirouetting gean
for her deep kiss in their
high cerulean bliss – know

this, that you are Mine,
who shaped those lips.

ii

Remember Rotterdam. Childbirth beneath the tiered tower. Red stone clearly recalls all that went before, right back to the monastery. Always one church by grace untouched amidst the conflagration chants into litany each scorched deserted street. All war begins with insolence, first stone thrown in the face of immense impartiality. How to relate this history? Look, our own names engraved upon the plinth, how grandiose!

what is here uplifted, raised? a
city bold but pitifully holed – gaze
on memoryless rain, the little
truths we leave untold, common
touch of friend and foe – broken
child, find a fragment of your past,
lay it here on the orphaned quay

City of memento mori: bronze bear cubs frolic on the mall, the little ballerina in museum park denies her pain, dreaming *en pointe* in bloodied tulip bed. At the waterside stood ruination's cry flung up into dread-laden skies. Who rent apart this ribcage, on whose side was the warrior who looted it, discarded the eviscerated heart? Here where the shell-shocked citizen stooped to rebuild, retrieve a rubbled edge of cornerstone. Pity the misled pilot for his velvet-couched desire.

iii

I looked around for rule of law, or thumb. One or other should be perceptible, I thought. A number of discordant voices trespassed on my mind. It was hard to know who was in charge. Schismatic as Raskolnikov, I dreamt night after night of confiding guilt to inattentive listeners, all unperturbed. Worst was my mariticide, of which they swore they had never heard.

our guardian, my love, or
angel, if you will, plain as
Pasolini's, and always tousled
red, nothing much to say,
but one day suddenly at
the greengrocer's served
me your unspoken name

At last I reached the frontier, crossed, came to an open road. It was deserted. I read the one-word sign that repudiates refusal. Obvious there was no choice. After that it was a simple matter of the walk ahead, who one came across and so on. Mostly ciphers of the unmapped habitat, now and then the same interventionist; limpid-eyed shower of the way, laconic, afro-haloed, bold.

iv

Saudade, desiderium, *heimwei, ûnwenne*: pining for what is gone, remembrance of pleasure, presence. Desolation duplicitous, half yearning to speak, half sour-sweet severance of the tongue. Or sometimes a sort of homesickness, vague longing for some other where or thing, irretrievable, already here. I found myself inhabiting a vast and stupendous simplicity. Walk, discover destination in the next step. Wait, stretch time into space. Find no answer there.

some lessons in emptiness:
one – wakefulness of water
two – straight course between reeds
three – grace in tempest
four – unasked intimacy
five – cold reason
six – bitter season

First want and then war. What is missing, missed that must be won. Yet what if fight itself be slain, overcome, overlain, subsumed beneath careening teleology? Who has lost sight of all cause and consequence, who? This is a merciful madness. Enforced jettisoning of the knife. Bring me to the close of day, dear god. Bring him close.

v

Because she holds him to her heart, All-Holy Virgin the Kardiotissa miraculously comes to me. Virgin Theotokos of the Passion, later rechristened Our Lady of Perpetual Succour, gilded *estofado* on sun-wooed Cretan rosewood. Wonder-worker painted by St. Lazaros, picked up in an old highland antique shop for next to nothing. Stolen, too, lifted at some unhinged moment from her red-brick Herculean monastery, detained for seven centuries by girl-child visionary in Rome. Scandalous, the stilled sojourn of the abductee, their unframed soliloquy.

exquisite, that light clasp, miniscule
fists about her thumb, his sandal
dangling by broken strap from bare
instep – see how he looks away from
foretold fate, fair rationale in disarray –
corrects skewed equilibrium, offers
excuse for meagre hold on truth

Pinned to the veil above her brow a gold Star of the Sea, the name the desert fathers gave the girl who drowns in prayers unceasingly. How grave his eyes that read the signs of sponge and lance, triple-branched tree. How brave her calm repose, strong hands, sharp folds of fortune in her clothes.

vi

Decades I dreamt I missed the boat, unable to embark, delayed by pity on the quay, hindered by care, complicity. A call to nurse or meet some other urgent need, obey lifelong unwritten law. Stalked by the family whose stridor I'd discerned, a breathless duty left undone I'd find myself in the underground, the same tunnel time and again, or pacing the same platform where the same train refused to run.

at the school gate childhood
waits – dies with the unfound
face, an absent hand that held
it to itself, empties its eyes of
hide-and-seek – stares at adult
fear, its blind swipe at rain on
playtime's tear-stained cheek

Day came when I cancelled the crossing. Outraged at farewell pallor on the morning playground I phone, postpone return ticket in breach of agreed access plan. All day wandering the streets. One of those English towns, so undaunted somehow. Smug culture of the colonist. Shops that never close, never run out of reason. Trees, always, in neat avenues. Awaiting afternoon at half past three. Bud-break on his introrse astonished face.

vii

As though adultery were not mute enough, we lost the art of conversation. Nothing to say at unasked violation of the peace, struck dumb by triple hit from nowhere. Three dispossessed and nothing to be done but divvy up the silence. Bewilderment on each estranged beloved face as space and time ballooned between us and hatred grew among the cobblestones, began to bloom and spread until no word more could be said.

we had need of Solomon's sabre
– what is love but want of might
to wield the cleaver? he lay between
us like some speechless mite long-
lost from history while judges heard
thrice times anew his solemn wish
whispered amid the maelstrom

Faith having arrived unasked, I wondered how one lost it. Perhaps erasure by turpitude, or simply careless misplacement. Act of revenge on grace that led to pain? Maybe god-given as release from laws impossible to keep, or catharsis, sudden renunciation. I gave thought to self-sacrifice in a good cause. For how long could the hunger striker survive refusing even water? Life it seemed sustained itself on far lesser fare than evidence.

viii

North-east I walked into the wind. Flat pastureland, nowhere to hide, time and again they told me this, such native pride. Curds like clotted sea-ice shivering in brine, cat lap beneath the vat, truckles filled with fat golden wheels turned week by week by weathered son while mother cheesemaker knits her finger-spun undyed, straight from the fleece. Time ripened need, siloed the free.

your voice, my sweet boy, your
mislaid sound – your face, my
irreplaceable – where are you
taken? ground strewn with high
summer's toys, curlew's curved
alarm bannering a nested clutch,
descant to lapwing's clamour

Although kindly in intent, this land of unrestrained horizons held me to a single coordinate as on and on the traverse led through unmastered incompetence. The ordered world was in rapid retreat, becoming more remote from me than hostage from home. I could not think where he might be.

ix

Remember? first-floor apartment in leafy pre-war Delfshaven (how it was spared nobody knows – remember Isaac, whose father sold bananas on the market, 1942, whole families routed from home, trucked, assembled for deportation in the harbour), a quiet little port on the Maas where that great river weds the Rhine. A quietly dying marriage in city of resurrections. Crazy, all that new architecture! especially the tilting cubes, one too many *Leffes* and *Oudes* at Jazz Café Dizzy. But when the peacetime bombshell came it shook the watchtower two kilometres away, trembled crocuses in the park. Spring holiday, a first birthday. Thirteen more to come before the third stern summons, father and son in steerage overnight, and meanwhile all the same old sins of commission and omission.

krokusvacantie – conclaves of
small purpura priests serve Pascal
mass at feet of towered heathen
hoards – pray for the estuary
that storms toward epiphany, ask
how to pilot the human heart, its
wild cargo of philotimo, smart

Triage being an inexact science we miss the subtle sign, betray life's feint, abandon hope. Make for the door with whatever we can salvage. Dream of a second honeymoon. Depart for a short break. Source the right kit with which to garb distraction. Alpine forest, rain, glimpse of eclipsed escape, lost height, night's commonplace displacement. O my abandoned wordless child whose veiled eyes teem with holy writ. Some destinies are inescapable. He soon mastered spatio-temporal solitude, the vital need for refuge. Pencils and bricks. Little doors and roofs and windows.

x

I knew that in this case the only rights were his, certainly none mine. The way I read it, no philosophy had quite defined the premise. All claim appalled me. Impossible, the untangling of human dues. Imponderable, when each year accrued drew my mind still farther out from certainty. Nourished wants and needs and weaknesses that fostered communality but kept me more and more locked into me.

night-swathed slave to man-made law
shortcuts through the *hoerenbuurt*
to court, vermilion-lipped, determined
but discreet enough to shudder stars
with her straight speech – wrests waylaid
desire from thrawn embrace, becalms
and entenders, entrusts to other arms

Late afternoon, I see him, glimpsed for the first time permitted that day, waiting quite alone in a dimly lit high-ceilinged atrium outside the courtroom. Waiting for her to emerge and tell him the verdict. Tall, thin, fragile, barely grown custodian of nothing but his right to life and where to place it. How he had waited. How later that cold darkening evening he laid his small backpack quietly beside us in the train, a change of clothes or two packed for a week's holiday. How close we sat together on that journey north, and hardly spoke. No words for then, the not yet distant catastrophe, a sorrowing solitude at sea. For the unmitigated joy of now, and unending tomorrow.

Notes

baklava
Socrates' mother was a midwife. Both Greece and Turkey have always claimed to have invented the delicacy made of layered filo pastry, honey and crushed nuts known as 'baklava' or 'placenta'. In ancient Rome it was known as 'placenta cake'. On the island of Lesbos it is today called simply 'placenta'.

face
The original Repulse Bay Hotel in southern Hong Kong, built overlooking the bay in 1920 and renowned recreational retreat of royalty and Hollywood celebs, was demolished in 1982 to make way for a new high-rise luxury apartment building. The Feng Shui Master consulted by the architects for feasibility on their new site development forbade any prospective building high enough to obstruct entry and exit to its home in the mountain for the resident dragon. The resulting complex overlooking the bay therefore features a massive 'hole' at its heart, allowing the dragon to freely come and go.

Gwailou: white foreigner, 'white ghost', 'white devil' (Cantonese).

Laura
Laura: the fragile girl character, based on his sister, in Tennessee Williams' play *The Glass Menagerie* (1944), who collects spun-glass animals and suffers ceaseless pressure from her dominant mother for her to find a husband.

A Minor Planet
A 'minor planet' may be a star that is neither a planet nor a comet; since 2006 covering dwarf planets and small solar-system bodies. In 1977 minor planet 3461 was named after the poet Osip Mandelstam, and in 1982 minor planet 3511 was designated 'Tsvetaeva'.

Oracle
The Oracle, also known as the Pythia, whose sacred shrine was at Delphi on Mount Parnassus in Ancient Greece, is said to have prophesied there from as early as 1400 BC. Her oracles in hexameter have been called 'the last fragment of Greek poetry which has moved the hearts of men' (J. B. Bury, *History of the Later Roman Empire* 2 1 (London 1931) 370; F. W. H. Myers, in Evelyn Abbot, *Hellenica 2* (London 1898) 447.) The choice of a young virgin as Pythia was abandoned after such were proven sexually vulnerable. Hereafter, an older

woman was chosen, who then left marital home and children in order to live at the shrine; the habit continued of Pythia dressing as a young woman. Kings, warriors and commoners consulted her for advice, and even Apollo himself sought her counsel. Her cryptic prophesy was often misinterpreted, especially when a negative outcome was forecast, but was always retrospectively seen to have been accurate. The early Christian era saw confusion engulf the Oracle, whose female power and authority were deeply revered yet perceived as a threat by the new cult religion; a dichotomy the repercussions of which were promptly divined by the Pythia. Successive Roman emperors attempted either to reinstate a degraded Oracle or to destroy it. Finally, Julian (ruled 361–363 AD) sent an emissary to Delphi to rebuild the shrine, only to be rewarded with Pythia's last utterance: 'Tell the emperor that the Daidalic hall has fallen. No longer does Phoebus have his chamber, nor mantic laurel, nor prophetic spring – and the speaking water has been silenced.'

Decalogue

No consensus exists within Christianity as to the order or wording of the Ten Commandments. Kieślowski was Polish and a Catholic, but his *Decalogue* film sequence follows no particular enumeration. This was surely a deliberate decision on his part, expressing the random individual and circumstantial interpretation and response to moral imperative. My sequence adopts the original Decalogue according to the Hebrew Bible as this seemed most comprehensively and chronologically accommodating of my narrative:

1. I am the lord your God who brought you out of the land of Egypt… the house of bondage.
2. You shall have no other gods beside Me. You shall not make for yourself or worship any graven image.
3. You shall not take the name of the Lord your God in vain.
4. Remember the Sabbath, to keep it holy.
5. Honour your father and your mother.
6. You shall not murder.
7. You shall not commit adultery.
8. You shall not steal.
9. You shall not bear false witness against your neighbour.
10. You shall not covet your neighbour's house… nor any thing that is your neighbour's.

ii Ossip Zadkine's monumental bronze, *The Destroyed City*, commemorates the razing of mediaeval Rotterdam by enemy and allied bombardment in 1940 and 1942, respectively.

iii Film director Pier Paolo Pasolini in his masterpiece *The Gospel According to St Matthew* cast an unknown Italian peasant as the guiding angel, an androgynous being with a lovingly dispassionate gaze beneath a wild mass of curls.

iv *heimwee*: homesickness (Dutch).
ûnwenne: homesickness (Frisian).

v Icon of the miraculous All-Holy Virgin the Kardiotissa, painted by a fourteenth-century monk of the Keros Kardiotissas monastery on Crete during the period of the Iconoclasm and a century later smuggled to Rome and adopted by the Catholic Church; her monastery is now a nunnery where the birthday of the Theotokas is celebrated every year on 8th September.

vii The Judgement of Solomon, Hebrew Bible, 1 Kings 3: 16-28

ix *krokusvacantie*: Spring half-term school holiday, in the Netherlands named for the first spring flowers.

philotimo (from the Greek: *philos* – friend, *timi* – honour): the all-embracing deep-seated impetus in us to do good, honour others.

A listed monument and the highest building in the Netherlands, the modernist Euromast observation tower was designed by Hugh Maaskant for the 1960 horticulture show, the Floriade, in Het Park on Rotterdam's Maas boulevard.

Leffe: strong Belgian beer
Oude: old (matured) Jenever, Dutch gin drunk as shots.

x *hoerenbuurt*: Red-light district (Dutch).

www.ingramcontent.com/pod-product-compliance
Lightning Source LLC
Chambersburg PA
CBHW030048100426
42734CB00036B/581